Freddie and the Steam Trains

Book 1: Early Days

David Lloyd

authorHOUSE®

AuthorHouse™ UK Ltd.
500 Avebury Boulevard
Central Milton Keynes, MK9 2BE
www.authorhouse.co.uk
Phone: 08001974150

First published by AuthorHouse 7/25/2011

ISBN: 978-1-4490-7025-0 (sc)

Contents

Acknowledgements

I would like to offer my sincere thanks to my wife Gloria, my son Matthew and to my friend Bill Oates PA for their support and encouragement in writing this book. My thanks also to the Bluebell Railway and Kent and East Sussex Railway for the railway photograph opportunities for this book.

Dedication

I would like to dedicate this book to all the volunteers on Heritage Railways across the British Isles, past, present and future, especially the young men and ladies who will keep them steaming for generations to come. As the General Manager of the Kent and East Sussex Railway my well used quote was, *"There is nothing stronger than the heart of a volunteer"* it is true. Thank you, this book is for you!

Chapter 1
Early days

Freddie awoke with a start; it was his Mother calling him. "Come on Freddie," she said. "Its 6.30 and you have got your interview on the railway today." Freddie sat up and rubbed his tired eyes, then recalled he had been unable to fall asleep the night before because of his excitement.

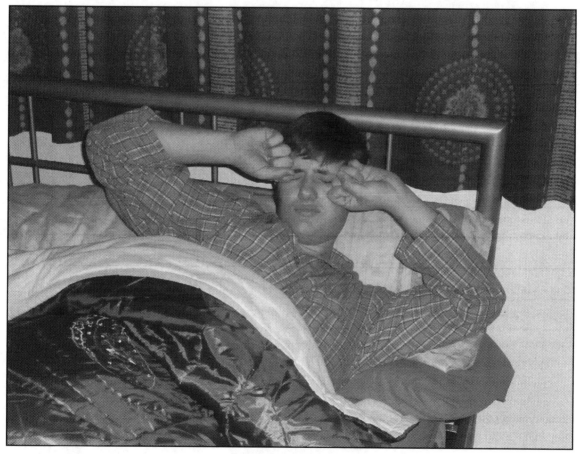

Freddie wakes up

Freddie had lain in bed remembering his schooldays and holidays standing by the railway crossing gates in the village of Wye where he lived, watching the steam trains either, racing through the station or, stopping on their way to London.

It was only a village station but it had its own shunting yard and the engines would come to a stop right across the road and often he was hidden by steam as they slowly left the station. Freddie would watch as people got off the trains on their way to the Wye racecourse.

Inside the signalbox

Sometimes he would wait for his Gran who would return from shopping in Ashford. At Christmas they would go for a train ride to Canterbury to listen to carols in the Cathedral and would stop off for hot roasted chestnuts on the way back to the station. Freddie would then enjoy returning back to Wye Station and watching as the engine pulled away.

There was also the signal box on the station, with red, yellow and black levers and all sorts of bells sounding. Freddie would be allowed into the signal box on some mornings when he took Uncle George the Signalman his breakfast, Aunty Cis would wrap the breakfast in a tea towel and if steam came from his bacon and eggs and it was still hot when he took the cloth off Freddie would receive 2d.

When Freddie went to secondary school in Ashford there was a big main line station with large shunting yard called the sorting sidings. It was just over the fence from the school playing fields, so close he could hear the Shunters calling out to the Engine Crews and Guards.

Freddie got in trouble one day watching the trains go by, he played for the school football team and they were playing against their arch rivals.

He was the goalkeeper and his team was on the attack at the other end of the field. Freddie heard the whistle of a train coming through the station and watched it go past. He was distracted by a lot of shouting and looking up the football pitch saw his team pointing to him. He looked around and the football was in the back of his goal, the other team had scored when he had been watching the trains go by.

The Sports Master Mr Guppy was not amused and would say to Freddie, "Are you playing football today or watching trains?"

Freddie didn't get on very well with English, Maths, History or Geography as the classrooms overlooked the railway and he was always watching trains and missed most of the lessons.

Express passenger train

In the summer months his Mother would allow him to visit the West Yard where the coal wagons would be emptied by the local coal merchants, but his favourite place was by the cattle docks. The Ashford market was nearby and the cattle and sheep would be unloaded from the cattle trucks and into the market to sell. Freddie also went to the Hump Yard where he would watch the engine push the trucks slowly over a little hill; the Shunter would uncouple the trucks he wanted with a long pole.

The Shunter would then tell the Driver to stop, but the uncoupled trucks would carry on. Another Shunter would make sure the points were set and send them onto other trucks which they would bump into with a big bang; it was very exciting and noisy.

Engine taking water

Next to the Hump Yard was the Locomotive Shed, this was the real place to be. Freddie would sit on the wall with many other boys writing down the train numbers in his note book.

There were passenger engines, tank engines, freight engines and sometimes express engines. Fast trains would race through the station some with flags on the front and Pullman coaches behind.

They would all need coal and water and many went onto a large turntable and were turned round by the Driver and Fireman.

Ashford station had 4 platforms and two fast lines through the middle. From platform 1 which was a bay platform you could go to Hastings, Dover or Canterbury. Platform 2 was the up platform to Tonbridge, Maidstone and London. Platform 3 was the down platform to Dover, and Canterbury, and platform 4 was another bay platform used for local trains to Canterbury, Ramsgate and Hastings.

Some other sidings went off from the Hastings line to the general goods siding and Locomotive Works where engines were built and repaired. The Gate Keeper would never allow Freddie to have a look round so, a once a year visit on the works open day was all he could expect.

Freddie would stand on the end of the platform 3 where the big green express engines stopped, he would watch the Fireman climb onto the top of the loco and pull the big pipe that was hanging from a tower then put it into the tank. The Driver would then turn a wheel and water would gush into the tank until it was full.

All of these trains had come from London and would be going to Folkestone, Dover and Ramsgate.

Footplate of engine

Sometimes a kind Driver would invite him onto the footplate and Freddie would see the many handles and gauges, he would smell the coal and oil and hear the hissing of the steam from the boiler and pipes, then feel the heat from the huge fire burning in the firebox.

"Come on mate," the Driver would say. "Off you get we are leaving now." Freddie would then obediently but begrudgingly climb down from the engine footplate and watch as the Driver and Fireman prepared to leave, sometime shovelling coal on to the fire, sometimes checking the gauges and turning the handles. They would then look out and watch the signals as they were ready to depart.

Ready to depart

Freddie would watch the train go with the red semaphore signal partly raised showing a green light telling the Driver it was safe to go over the mass of rails and points that lay ahead.

As the train left Freddie would watch the red signal come crashing down until it was horizontal showing a red light telling the next driver he must stop. It was because Freddie had seen, heard, smelt and felt all these things as a young boy that he had always wanted to be an Engine Driver and now his chance had come.

Signals

Chapter 2
Interview and a start date

Freddie was the eldest of two children he was just coming up to being 15 years old, his Brother Brian was 11. His Grandmother also lived with them as her house had been hit during the war by a flying bomb called a doodlebug. As the eldest Freddie had many responsibilities at home. The garden was an allotment which he dug and planted vegetables in. At the end of the garden there was a chicken house and run which housed 11 chickens from which they had sufficient eggs for their needs. Freddie got up and went out to complete his chores before leaving.

Freddie working in the garden

Mother saved all the potato peelings and vegetable scraps they would be boiled, the mixture was then mashed and corn bran added. With a handful of corn this was the chicken's diet on which they thrived.

Freddie would sell any surplus eggs and vegetables and use the money to buy bran and corn.

His Father had no interest in gardening but his Uncle Jim gave him advice and vegetable plants. His Father's current job was as the Works Manager in the army engineering works in Ashford. He often brought home large tins of corned beef, fruit, dried eggs and powdered milk which were no longer required for the army lorries and tanks.

Mother would work miracles with the corned beef and with fresh vegetables from the garden they would eat well. "Can you pick some vegetables for dinner before you get changed Freddie," Mother asked.

Freddie picking vegetables

Mother also made all their bread and made jam of which there was always plenty.

Brian helped in the garden at times but he was always studying mathematics and was very good at school work. This pleased Father as being an engineering mathematician himself could help Brian with his algebra and fractions.

Father, Freddie and Brian

However, Brian was also a bad boy, always in trouble, he had been very ill as a baby with stomach trouble but made up for it now by eating everything in sight, yet he was very skinny.

Freddie looked at the clock, it was time for him to get changed, he didn't want to be late.

Freddie's school had arranged for Freddie to fill out an application form and attend an interview at Ashford Railway Station.

His father was not impressed that Freddie was going to the railway as he was a clever engineer and had wanted Freddie to follow him in the same line of work.

Freddie's Mother made sure he was smart with a white shirt and a tie which she had borrowed from Father's collection.

"Clean your shoes," Mother said. "You need to look your best."

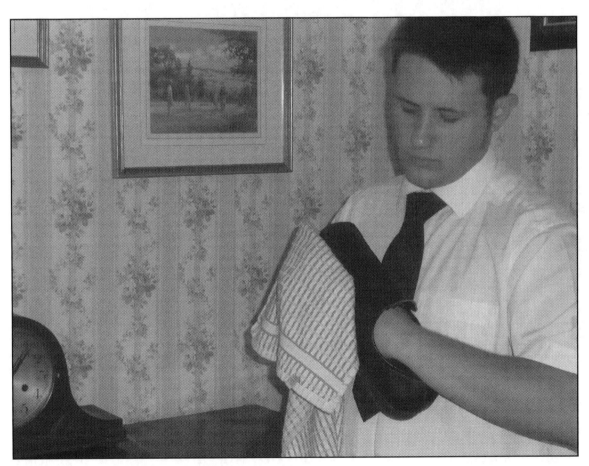
Freddie polishes his shoes

Freddie arrived at the Railway Station with time to spare and sat in a waiting room with other candidates some of which he attended school with.

First they had a medical to make sure they were fit and healthy then they sat once again in the waiting room.

One by one they were called into another room and soon Freddie's name was called out. He went into the room closed the door and saw two men showing only the tops of their heads sitting at a desk writing on pieces of paper.

"Sit down," one of them said without looking up, Freddie did as he was told.

Eventually they finished writing and both looked up, they had really serious faces and staring eyes. One had a very thin face, with ginger hair brushed to one side, the other had dark hair.

Why do you want to join the railway?" The thin face man asked.

"To be an Engine Driver," Freddie replied.

"Do you think you could drive an engine?" The dark haired man asked.

"No not yet," Freddie said.

"Do you know how old you have to be to become a Driver?" the thin faced man asked.

"No," Freddie replied.

"Twenty three," the dark haired man said. "Do you still want to start on the railway?"

Freddie felt suddenly empty inside, he thought he was going to be driving a train next week, but without thinking further.

Freddie said, "Yes sir, I do want to work on the railway."

Freddie being interviewed

The dark haired man then explained to Freddie he would be cleaning engines for one year until he was 16. He would then go to the railway school to learn about the way engines worked and how to actually keep the fire as it should be. After that, he would be trained on engines and eventually passed out to be a fireman on local and goods trains.

"When will I be able to be a Fireman on the big expresses?" Freddie asked.

"Perhaps in about 5 years," the thin faced man replied. "You will start next Monday, 30th October at 08.00 finishing at 17.00, with one hour for lunch break."

"Your wages will be 35 shillings (£1-70) per week payable one week in arrears. You will work a 44 hour week your days off will be every Sunday and every other Saturday. All your clothing will be provided but you clean it yourself," the thin faced man explained.

"Any questions?" The dark haired man asked.

"Yes," Freddie said.

Slowly they looked at each other, then at Freddie and said together "What?"

"Where do I go on Monday morning?" Freddie asked.

"Report to the office in the locomotive shed," the thin faced man replied. "Goodbye."

Freddie went home feeling a little strange, he had got the job he wanted, but being able to drive a train seemed such a long way away.

Then he was met at home with bad news.

"Freddie come and sit down son," Mother said. "I have got something to tell you."

"As you know your Father has been working for the government since before the War and they now want him to go to a position in the aircraft industry. We are going to have to go with him," Mother said. "We are moving to a village called Abbots Langley in Hertfordshire, it is just outside Watford."

"What about my job on the railway?" Freddie asked.

"You will have to find another job, we are moving at the end of the week," Mother said.

Freddie receives bad news

Chapter 3
The move and a new start

Freddie went to bed in tears full of sadness, he had been able to get the job he wanted and now the opportunity was being taken from him because of his Father's work. At tea time his Father said, "Never mind I expect I can get you an apprenticeship with the aircraft company."

"I don't want a job with the aircraft company, I want to work on the railway," Freddie replied.

"Well that's too bad," Father said.

Freddie went to the locomotive offices the next day and told the Clerk what had happened.

The Clerk said, "Where is the nearest station to where you are going to live?"

Freddie told him.

The Clerk said, "Wait a minute while I make a telephone call."

When he returned the Clerk said, "If you go to the Watford Junction Station, and see the Station Master he will speak to the Locomotive Office Clerk and he may be able to help you."

"Thanks," Freddie replied and ran off to get the train home.

Mother was not very happy when Freddie explained what had happened, "your Father will not be pleased, he wants you to follow him into engineering," she said.

Mother was right, Father was not happy and said, "How will you get to the station?"

"On my cycle," Freddie replied.

"What? That old cycle it will fall to bits half way to the station," Father said laughing.

Freddie could see this was not going in the direction he had hoped for so he went out to say goodbye to his friends.

Friday came and the removal lorry arrived. The boxes they had packed were loaded with the furniture and off they went.

It was nearly ninety miles to their new home and Freddie sat behind the Driver with his Mother, Brother and Gran. The journey took 4 hours as they had to go through London.

Freddie found London exciting with so many buses and taxis, and crossing the River Thames over Vauxhall Bridge was the best part of the journey.

They arrived at their new home and soon sorted everything out. Freddie's younger brother Brian needed help, but all he had in mind was "hurry up Monday so I can go to the station and try to find work."

Freddie had worked for several years delivering groceries and gardening with his Uncle Jim and had saved up just over £16.

His Uncle Jim had been like a second Father to him as his own Father had been away from home working for the government.

He made the decision, if he managed to join the railway he would buy a new cycle.

Freddie's Uncle Jim with his old lorry

Monday arrived at last and off Freddie went to the station.

He found the office of the Station Master and explained what had happened in Ashford. The Station Master made a telephone call to the Locomotive Office Clerk who asked Freddie to go and see him.

Freddie was over the bridge in seconds and told the Clerk in the locomotive office who he was.

"Wwwwwwwwwait in the mmmmmmess room," the Clerk said. "I wwwwwwwwwill tell the ssssssshedmaster you are here."

Freddie went into the mess room where there was a big stove burning and the biggest kettle he had ever seen steaming on the top. He noticed on one side of the mess room there was a long table with a bench either side.

On one side sat four older men and on the other side two younger men who appeared to be a similar age to him.

Freddie learnt later the Drivers sat one side and the Firemen and Cleaners the other, and as a Fireman or Cleaner you never sat on the Driver's side unless invited, and that was not often.

The Clerk called Freddie out into the passageway and said, "tttttttthe sssssssshedmaster will ssssssee you now, call him MMMMMMMMMr Dodds."

Freddie knocked on his door and a loud voice said, "Come in". Freddie entered and Mr Dodds said. "Sit down and tell me what happened to you on the Southern Region."

After Freddie explained, Mr Dodds said, "Would you like to join the London Midland Region instead?"

Freddie was so excited, he could not get the words "yes please" out quick enough.

"Right," said Mr Dodds. "You will not need another interview or medical, you can start tomorrow if you would like to."

"Like to," Freddie thought "I would love to". "Yes please," he replied.

"Your hours of work and wages will be the same as you were told on the Southern Region," Mr Dodds continued. "See you sharp at 08.00," Mr Dodds added, and off Freddie went.

Freddie had seen a cycle shop earlier and now went there and purchased a new cycle with three gears and a dynamo hub for the cycle lights. It cost just under £10 brand new and that was with an insurance to cover any loss. The man even gave Freddie 10 shillings (50p) for his old bike, Freddie cycled home full of joy.

Chapter 4
The First day

Freddie leapt out of bed, washed and brushed his teeth and hair and went down for breakfast. Father never spoke to Freddie that morning he kissed Mother goodbye and went off to work, it was only a 10 minute walk to the airfield for him.

"I have packed you a lunch with a bottle of water for you, and I will have a dinner ready for you tonight," Mother said.

Freddie kisses his Mother goodbye

"Thanks mum," Freddie said kissing her on the cheek and put his lunch in his bag. Freddie went to the shed carefully removed his new cycle and set off for his first day on the railway.

It was a 3 mile ride and on the way Freddie passed his Father walking to work. "See you tonight Dad," he called out as he passed but there was no reply.

The cycle was going well and Freddie was learning the gears which made the ride easy.

On arriving at the locomotive shed Freddie asked an old man sweeping the floor where he could put his cycle.

"Against the wall on number four road with all the others," the old man said. "Or, you can leave it in the cycle shed at the top of the steps but it will not be very safe there."

The problem was where was number four road? Freddie looked around in the gloom of the shed and spotted several cycles leaning against a wall and took a guess that this was the right place.

Freddie puts his cycle with the others

Freddie then went to the booking on point and told the Clerk who he was. "This disc," the Clerk said. "showing number 1140 on it, is yours; you must collect it when booking on and hand it back in when you book off. You will also need to show it when you collect your wages next week," he added. "I will introduce you to the Shed Foreman and other Cleaners, after that we will go to the stores and fit you out with clothing."

Booking on disc

They found the Shed Foreman telling one of the Cleaners off, the discussion ended with the Foreman clipping the Cleaner around the left ear.

The Foreman wore a smart railway jacket, waistcoat and black hat.

"My name is Bill Heath and you work for me, you can call me Mr Heath," he said.

Mr Heath wasn't a big man but Freddie was frightened of him, Freddie did not want to experience his ear clipping right hand, seeing someone else receive it was enough.

"Go and get kitted out and meet me by 80064," Mr Heath said.

Off Freddie went with the Clerk to the stores and was issued with three sets of bib and brace overalls, three overall jackets, a rain coat and railway hat that had a shiny peak and shiny top.

"Do I get a badge for the hat?" Freddie asked the Clerk.

"When you pass out as a Fireman," the Clerk replied, "unless someone gives you an old one. Here you go lad have one of mine, now off you go and find Mr Heath your lunch break is 12.30 to 13.30."

"Thank you," Freddie said. "Can I ask you something?"

"Yes of course," the Clerk replied.

"What is 80064?" Freddie asked.

"It's a tank engine on number three road," the Clerk said.

"Thanks," said Freddie and went to meet Mr Heath who, called him onto the footplate and explained that 80064 was in the shed for boiler washout.

"Change into your overalls, one of the Cleaners will show you where the cleaning materials are," Mr Heath said. "I want you to clean the wheels and motions, I will return later to see how you are progressing." He then went off in the direction of the office.

Freddie looked at the 5 foot 8 inch wheels, which were slightly bigger than he was and then saw there were three of them connected by big metal rods, with one smaller wheel at the front and two smaller wheels at the back, and that was only on this side of the engine.

Billy Bailey was the Senior Cleaner and he introduced the other Cleaners whose names were Pete, Johnny, Paul and Joe he then showed Freddie where the materials were.

Cleaning the slide bars

"Fill the bucket half full of paraffin from this tank," Billy said, pointing to a tank labelled paraffin. "Then put in a little oil from this tank," Billy continued, pointing to another tank labelled oil. "Then take one of these brushes and give it a good mix, you are now ready to start work," he finished.

The brush was fitted to a cut down broom handle about 18 inches long. Freddie returned to the locomotive and began work.

"Dip the brush into the bucket then wash off the dirt in a scrubbing motion," Billy explained.

Weeks of oil, dust and grime had accumulated on the wheels but using plenty of paraffin mix slowly the wheels began to show there was black paint underneath.

Cleaning the wheels

Chapter 5
In Trouble

The Cleaners had a break at 10.00 then continued working until lunch break by which time Freddie had finished one side of the engine, it looked nice and clean and Freddie was pleased with himself.

Sitting in the mess room eating lunch was really exciting as he listened to Drivers and Fireman telling stories of duties they had covered.

The mess room suddenly fell silent and Freddie was aware of someone standing by him and then someone's hand grabbed hold of his left ear and pulled him to my feet.

"Come with me lad," Mr Heath said.

Freddie was marched with his ear firmly clamped in Mr Heath's fingers to the side of 80064 which he had cleaned.

"What can you see wrong with your work?" asked Mr Heath.

"Nothing," Freddie replied.

"Well, look closely then," Mr Heath said twisting Freddie's ear a little bit more, Freddie looked but it all looked clean to him.

"I can't see what is wrong," Freddie cried out to which Mr. Heath said. "Stop whimpering you are not in any pain yet."

Suddenly the grip on his ear was released when a voice called out.

"Stop bullying that boy Bill he only started work today," it was Bill Sales the man who washed the boilers out.

"When two pieces of metal rub together what happens?" Mr Heath said.

Freddie had been taught metal work at School so he looked at Mr Heath and said, "They get hot."

"Good, how can we prevent them getting hot?" Mr Heath asked.

"Keep them cool," Freddie replied.

"On a steam locomotive, what could we use?" asked Mr Heath.

Freddie thought for a moment and nearly said steam but then he remembered all the oil he had put on his cycle to keep it running smoothly. He had been cleaning oil and grease off the wheels and motions all morning.

"Oil," Freddie said.

"Good, let us look at the cross head," said Mr Heath.

What was he talking about Freddie thought what is a cross head. Mr Heath took Freddie to the front of 80064 and said, "This large piece of metal is pushed to and fro by the piston, it slides between these two pieces of metal very fast. "Do you think it needs oil on it?"

"Yes," Freddie replied.

"Well why have you removed all the oil on the slide bars with paraffin?" Mr Heath asked.

"I thought I had to clean all the motions like you said," Freddie replied.

Freddie tried to duck, but it was too late, Mr Heaths hand caught him on top of the head and he staggered back.

Freddie points at the cross head

"Don't try and be funny," Mr Heath said. "Go and have your lunch then put oil on the slide bars and don't use paraffin in that area again."

When Freddie returned to the mess room the other Cleaners fell about laughing.

"We just had a bet you had cleaned the slide bars," Billy said.

"But you told me to clean everything," Freddie said. "You must have watched me when you were cleaning the tanks and boiler casing."

"Of course," Billy said. "But we have all had a stinging ear from Stingem and wanted to see you get one on your first day."

"Who is Stingem?" Freddie asked.

"Bill Heath," Billy answered. "But don't let him hear you call him that."

"Thanks very much," was all Freddie could say then tucked into his cheese and pickle sandwiches.

Chapter 6
A Day Ends

After their lunch break the Cleaners returned to work then Freddie noticed that after about one hour he was the only one working on the engine, where had the other five Cleaners gone?.

Rather than risk the attention of Mr Heath he continued cleaning the wheels and motions taking great care not to allow any paraffin onto the slide bars.

After finishing the wheels and cab side he climbed onto the footplate and cleaned the various pipes and gauges.

Freddie cleans 80064

It was about 16.45 when he finished and suddenly the other Cleaners returned they had been missing over two hours.

"Where have you been?" Freddie asked.

"Has Stingem been round?" Johnny asked.

"No," Freddie replied.

"Good," said Johnny. "We have been to the cinema up the road, Paul's dad is the Manager there and he allows us to watch the big film that starts at 2.20pm."

"What would I have done if Mr Heath had come round asking where you were?" Freddie asked.

"He never comes round on a Tuesday or Thursday afternoon he visits his mum in hospital," explained Billy. "Except sometimes he changes his visiting days and that may catch us out, that's why we left you behind."

The Cleaners all went to the washroom and cleaned the dirt and grease off their hands and faces. Freddie then handed in his disc to the man he first met when he had come to the locomotive shed for a job.

"Hhhhhhhhhow was your ffffffffffffffirst day?" the Clerk asked.

"Very interesting," Freddie said.

"Did Stingem cccccccccccatch up with you?" the Clerk inquired.

"Yes," Freddie replied touching his still sore head. The Clerk threw back his head and laughed and as he did so his top and bottom set of false teeth fell from his mouth, but his hand shot out and he caught them and in one swift movement replaced them in his mouth.

The clerk loses his false teeth

Freddie retrieved his cycle from number four road, carried it up the steps from the locomotive shed, pushed it up the alley to the main road then cycled home wearing his new railway hat, with the raincoat and spare overalls on the carrier. It was still light but Freddie was looking forward to using his new dynamo later when he went to Sea Cadets.

Father was already home and eating his dinner, and when mother saw the overalls and Freddie's still dirty face quickly sent him to the shed to remove the overalls and to the bathroom to clean up.

Sitting at the dinner table his younger brother Brian was eager to know what Freddie had been doing. After relating the day's events but leaving out the clipped ear. Father said, "You had better learn to wash properly there is enough dirt in your ears to grow potatoes in." Freddie was promptly sent back to the bathroom to wash.

Mother was upstairs at the time and using a flannel cleaned him up.

Freddie then realised washing would have to be different than before as the dirt really did get everywhere.

"I will not be able to wash your overalls by hand," Mother said. "But I will ask the co-op cleaners when they come round if they clean overalls."

"Thanks Mum," Freddie said. "Dad seems so angry when I am around."

"He wanted you to work with him but he will be alright if you do well," Mum replied.

Freddie returned to the dinner table to find his dinner had been finished by his brother Brian who seemed to eat everything in sight.

Brian eats the dinner left on the plate

Freddie then dressed in his Sea Cadets uniform and with his dynamo humming on the wheel cycled back into town, past the loco shed to the drill hall for an evening of study and practice. He had joined the Sea Cadets when he was twelve and had been going twice a week ever since. He found it hard going to a new unit but he would soon settle in.

What a day.

Chapter 7
Learning about the engines

The next day Freddie had another engine to clean 80037. It was not as dirty as the previous one and despite being given the wheels and motions again which all new Cleaners have to do, he began to enjoy the work and what went on around the locomotive shed.

It was not a big shed only six roads each of which had a deep pit underneath to allow access to the underside of the engines. Each road could hold three engines, but if one was a tender engine part of the engine would be out into the open.

Next to the shed was the ash pit road where the engines fires were cleaned, with all the ashes falling into a pit underneath.

Then there was the coaling area which was two roads. One rose steeply up and the full coal wagons were pushed up into the covered area.

The engines used the next road and were coaled by hand by the coaling staff who threw big lumps of coal into the bunker or tender, then when they reached the bottom of the wagon they could open the wagon side doors and shovel the coal into the bunker or tender.

The coaling area was brick built with an enormous water tank on the top holding 30,000 gallons of water for the engines.

Next to the coaling area was a turntable for turning the engines around. It was hand operated and was only big enough to turn the smaller of the tender engines, but could turn any size tank engine.

It was hand operated so needed at least two people to turn an engine.

It was possible to leave the loco either out across the branch line into the sidings or, onto the up slow line on the other side of the engine.

The highlight of the day was taking it in turns to go round by the side of the locomotive shed where the main line was and watch the expresses that stopped at the station leaving for the Midlands and North.

Two of the Cleaners who had been there for nearly a year even knew the class of the express engines, but at the moment they were just big engines to Freddie.

Wheels of an express engine

One day Freddie was sent to assist Bill Sales building a brick arch. This meant getting into the firebox through the firebox doors on the footplate which you could not do unless you were reasonably slim. The brick arch is actually made of special bricks that are slightly oval and they were built over a wooden template to ensure they were the right shape and in the right place.

The brick arch in the firebox prevents the fire from going directly out of the chimney and diverts the flame, smoke and heat so the boiler gets the best heat over its surface and so produces steam from the boiling water.

"Come on up matey," Bill said. "I will show you how it's done."

Bill Sales

Bill climbed into the firebox with an electric lamp and Freddie passed the bricks and tools through to him.

"Come on in matey," Bill said.

Bill and Freddie then began work in the confined space and suddenly the firebox doors slammed shut with them both inside.

There was a loud cheer followed by laughter as the culprit and his followers ran off leaving them trapped, it was not easy to open the firebox doors from the inside.

"Let's get on with it," Bill said. "They will open the doors when they are fed up with messing around."

Sitting on the firebox grate was reasonably comfortable and there was plenty of air coming through the grate. Bill was a good teacher and once he had the first row of bricks in place watched as Freddie put in the second row, guiding him when he went wrong, he then finished the final row and they were ready to go for a tea break.

Brick arch inside the firebox

"Where are you Bill?" a voice called out.

"Shut in the firebox matey," said Bill.

They heard the sound of someone climbing onto the footplate then, the firebox doors opened.

It was Frank Jolley who was the assistant to Bill Sales.

"Why did you shut the doors?" inquires Frank.

"We didn't," said Bill. "It was that idiot Pete he will regret and remember today when I have finished with him."

They climbed out and put the tools away and went for their break, Bill said, "Next week I will show you a boiler washout."

"Thank you," said Freddie.

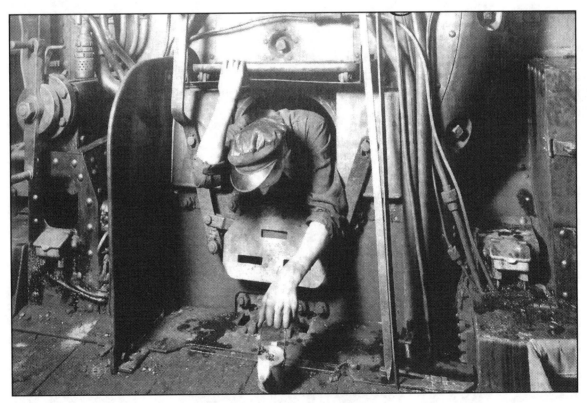

Climbing out of the firebox

This was also the end of Freddie's second week and he went to the rear of the station booking office, handed over his number 1140 disc and was given a little round tin with a lid on. He removed the lid and inside was £1-17s-6d (£1.85p) with a printed piece of paper showing his National Insurance and Income Tax deductions.

His first week's wages, it felt very good.

Freddie went home that evening feeling very rich. Mother wanted 10 shillings (50p) for board, and 2 shillings and 6d (12p) for the Co-op Cleaner.

The rest was his to spend or save he was actually getting paid for what he always wanted to do.

First weeks wages

Chapter 8
Learning more and other dirty jobs

The following week Freddie was assisting Bill Sales on the boiler washout.

During a boiler washout a very high powered hose is used.

The boiler was already empty of water and was waiting to have the sludge washed out. This is achieved by removing the wash out plugs and mud hole doors.

Bill had a plan to have revenge on Pete for shutting them in the firebox.

The Cleaners were at work on a visiting engine on the next road and Pete was doing the wheels and connecting rod.

Bill very carefully lined up the hose and turned the handle to full on.

A jet of water shot from the nozzle on one side of the boiler, through one of the washout plugs on the other side and all over Pete.

Pete shouted, "What are you doing I am soaked?"

Bill replied, "Sorry matey I never saw you there."

At this point Mr Heath arrived on the scene.

"What are you doing Pete, messing about with water again?" Mr Heath asked.

"Nothing," said Pete. "It was Bill Sales."

Pete received a clip on the ear and Mr Heath said, "Have some respect for your elders and go to the mess room and change into something dry, and stop messing about with water."

Bill Heath looked at Bill Sales smiling, Freddie was told he didn't smile often "tut, tut, tut," he said. "I suppose that was for last week's firebox incident."

"How did you know about that?" Bill Sales asked.

"I know everything that goes on in the shed," Stingem replied. "Never forget that lad," he said to Freddie.

Some weeks later, Johnny and Freddie were sent to clear the ash pit. The ashes were three feet deep and when Freddie began to shovel them onto the side of the ash pit road, he found them still red hot and burning underneath. It was a case of cooling them down with a hose pipe, shovelling out then cooling down and so on.

When the pit was empty the shed crew shunted a wagon onto the ash road, Freddie now had to shovel the ashes into the wagon, which was easy to start with as the wagon doors were open, later it was much harder as when the doors were closed Freddie had to throw the shovel full of ashes nearly eight feet in the air over the wagon sides.

The dust covered Freddie from head to toe, the dust got in his eyes and ears, up his nose and inside his overalls, it was the worst job he ever had to do.

On another occasion Pete and Freddie were sent to coal a spare engine which had just come out of the shed following repairs. In the mornings the Coalers did not work they only covered the coaling area from 14.00 until 08.00 the following morning.

Sore hands

The work was hard as Freddie and Pete used their bare hands to throw large lumps of coal into the bunker. The coal came up from Wales and was known as Welsh soft coal, but it was not soft to handle and soon the Cleaner's hands were sore and bleeding.

Mr Heath thanked Pete and Freddie for their hard work and told them to wash up and have a long meal break; this was a new side to the Locomotive Foreman.

The Shed Turners duty was to move engines and wagons full of coal around the locomotive yard. As a special treat Pete and Freddie were told by Mr. Health that they could ride on the engine with the Shed Turner whilst he removed the wagons of ash, and put them into the siding.

They then returned from the siding with eight wagons of coal and pushed them up on to the coaling road ready to be used when needed.

Pete and Freddie were allowed to take turns to put coal on the fire and the Fireman showed them how to operate some of the equipment.

Freddie had never been allowed to ride on an engine before; they travelled out of the engine, across the St Alban's branch line, and into the shunting sidings.

The engine they used for the shunting was 44443, a Midland 4F. This was Freddie's best day yet and he recorded the engine number, the shunting and duty in his notebook.

He went home full of the things he had learnt, and been able to do, feeling full of excitement.

Chapter 9
Blue Eyed Boy

The following week Freddie was at work bright and early and had just finished a chore for Bill.

"Freddie," a voice called.

Freddie turned round and Mr Dodds the Shed Master was standing by his desk with his office door open.

"I want you to take some urgent papers to the head office at Euston," Mr Dodds said.

Pete and Johnny protested, "we, are senior to Freddie, we should go," they argued.

Freddie with rail pass and papers

"No," said Mr Dodds. "Freddie has clean overalls on and yours are dirty he needs to travel on the train."

"But," said Pete.

"No buts," said Mr Dodds. "Freddie goes."

The reason Freddie's overalls were usually fairly clean was because Mother had two sets collected on a Monday one week and one set the next week by the Co-op Cleaners and they were returned spotless on the Friday, all for two and sixpence (12p) per week.

Mr Dodds gave Freddie a rail pass and instructions to take some papers to a Mr McMillan at Euston.

Freddie made his way to platform 2 to catch the next electric to Euston.

"Do you want to ride up front with me?" asked Jack Butler the Driver.

Freddie knew Jack as he also worked in the locomotive office on some days acting as Foreman when Mr Heath was off duty.

"Yes please," Freddie said. "That would be great."

Freddie joined Jack in the cab of the old electric multiple unit and off they went.

This was the life sitting at the front of the train watching the green and red colour light signals.

Freddie couldn't believe that he was getting more and more opportunities to work on and travel on engines and units.

Jack explained many things on the way and the highlight was coming down the Camden bank and seeing the overhead signal showing a yellow light for caution and a large number 4 being displayed for platform 4.

At the offices Freddie found where Mr McMillan was located and delivered the papers as told.

"Would you like some tea and biscuits?" Mr McMillan asked.

"Yes please sir," Freddie answered. Mr McMillan poured some tea into a mug and placed it on the table with a plate of biscuits.

Drink and biscuits

"Help yourself to milk and sugar and eat all of the biscuits if you are hungry," he said.

"Thank you," Freddie replied.

Biscuits were an expensive item and rarely seen at home, mother made cakes and bread but not biscuits. Freddie ate all the biscuits and Mr McMillan told him to return to Mr Dodds and to thank him for the paper work.

Going back into the station Freddie looked at the board to see which train he could catch back to the Watford Junction, and saw a Wolverhampton train was leaving in 5 minutes first stop Watford Junction. Freddie went to platform 12 and made his way through the barrier. The ticket barrier staff took no notice as he was in overalls with a railway hat on.

Quickly Freddie went to the front of the train and saw it was a Royal Scot Class 46160 "Queen Victoria's Rifleman".

He wrote the details in his notebook and went into the leading Guard's area at the front of the first carriage and looked out of the window as the train left Euston and climbed the Camden bank.

Freddie had now been working as a Cleaner at Watford Locomotive Depot for several weeks and he rarely had time to sit and ponder how time had flown since his interview in Ashford and his start date the following week at Watford.

As Freddie listened to the train, he let himself drift off in to a day dream and imagined he was on the footplate with the Driver and the Fireman. He imagined he was shovelling coal onto the fire, checking the gauges and equipment, turning the handles, and pulling on the whistle. It felt like it would be years still before he would really be allowed to work on the mainline on the footplate with a Fireman.

Freddie looking out of the window

The roar from the chimney was something special and as the train passed the Camden Locomotive Depot Freddie saw rows of express engines waiting to go into service.

Freddie went inside the carriage and sat down, pressing his face against the window. As he watched the rails, he saw Bushey water troughs, that he had heard the Drivers and Fireman talk about in the mess room. "What are you doing in here?" a voice behind Freddie asked.

"Travelling back to Watford Junction," Freddie said to the Guard whom he now recognised in his smart uniform.

Express engine

"You are supposed to go on the electrics," the Guard said. "Have you got a pass?"

Freddie showed him his pass and said, "I have just been to see Mr McMillan with some important papers."

"Well if you have been doing a job for the boss, I suppose it's alright for you to travel with us," said the Guard.

Freddie often wondered if it wasn't alright how he would have got off before Watford Junction station.

The guard telling Freddie off

It was all a wonderful experience and Freddie was beginning to learn the parts of an engine and how they worked, he could see why he had to start at the bottom because there was so much to know before he could become a steam engine Fireman let alone a Driver.

As he was able to talk about different parts of an engine, Freddie found his Father was suddenly interested as it was engineering which his Father understood.

They had many interesting conversations at the dinner table. Freddie would explain how the valve gear worked and his Father would draw diagrams that showed the workings of an aircraft jet engine.

As the weeks passed into months Freddie understood there was a lot to learn.

Freddie and his Father studying

Bill Sales was always a willing teacher as was the Workshop Foreman Frank Beadle, Freddie wanted to learn and because he listened they spent time showing him. Mr Heath often allowed Freddie to assist Bill and Frank providing all the cleaning was finished.

When eight months had passed Freddie now became Senior Cleaner, Pete and Johnny had passed out as Firemen and were known as Passed Cleaners, some days they cleaned, other days they covered Fireman's duties. All the other Cleaners had left the railway to work in other places.

Freddie had five Cleaners to look after some would last a few days others would remain to become Fireman.

Mr Dodds was also giving Freddie lessons on the Rule Book in preparation for when he was sixteen and could attend the firing school at Willesden Junction.

Freddie was also promised that during his final six weeks prior to his birthday he would be allocated to a qualified Fireman and would cover the day duties on the footplate.

As Freddie worked in the new garden, turning the area into an allotment like the one he had in Wye and working with the chickens in the new chicken house and run he had built, he pondered the things he was learning in the rule book and from the many lessons he had received from the more senior men, he loved his job.

Freddie knew it was wrong to wish that time would go quickly, but the thought of actually being on an engine in passenger service, well, he couldn't wait.

The End